A New True Book

YELLOWSTONE

NATIONAL PARK

By David Petersen

CHILDRENS PRESS®

CHICAGO

Mammoth Hot Springs in Yellowstone
National Park

Project Editor: Fran Dyra
Design: Margrit Fiddle

*acc
8-13-90*

FIELDS CORNER

PHOTO CREDITS

© Reinhard Brucker—4 (bottom left), 6 (large photo), 7, 8, 19, 20, 21, 29, 30 (3 photos), 38 (bottom)

Camerique—23 (left)

© Virginia R. Grimes—23 (right)

Journalism Services—© Dave Brown, cover, 35

Kirkendall/Spring—2

© Raleigh Meade—12, 41 (2 photos)

North Wind Picture Archives—13, 15 (left)

© Rob Outlaw—4 (bottom right), 28

Root Resources—© James Blank, 14 (left);
© Mary A. Root, 34

Bob and Ira Spring—14, 18, 43, 44

Tom Stack & Associates—© Sharon Gerig, 33;
© Gerald & Buff Corsi, 38 (top left); © Brian Parker, 40 (top left); © Thomas Kitchin, 6 (left inset), 40 (bottom right); © Mary Clay, 42;
© Diane Stratton, 6 (right inset); © Spencer Swanger, 45

© Lynn M. Stone—4 (top), 16 (left), 36

SuperStock International, Inc.—© Edmond Van Hoorick, 10

TSW-CLICK/Chicago—© Raymond G. Barnes, 24

Valan—© Jean-Marie Jro, 27; © Dennis W. Schmidt, 16 (right); © Wayne Lankinen, 32, 38 (top right); © Stephen J. Krasemann, 40 (top right); © Jeff Foott, 40 (bottom left)

Linda Brodin—map on 15, illustration on 25

Cover—The lower falls of the Yellowstone River

Library of Congress Cataloging-in-Publication Data

Petersen, David.
  Yellowstone National Park / by David Petersen.
     p.   cm. — (A New true book)
  Includes index.
  Summary: An introduction to the national park best
known for its dramatic thermal features.
  ISBN 0-516-01148-0
    1. Yellowstone National Park—Juvenile literature.
[1. Yellowstone National Park.   2.   National parks
and reserves.] I. Title. II. Series.
F722.P48   1992
917.87′52—dc20   91-37292
                                                         CIP
                                                          AC

TABLE OF CONTENTS

Visitors to Yellowstone National Park can see the Grand Canyon
of Yellowstone (above) and Tower Fall (below left). People like to fish
for trout on the Madison River (below right).

A WORLD OF WONDERS

Out in Wyoming, there is a special place called Yellowstone National Park. The park takes its name from rhyolite, a yellow rock found there.

At Yellowstone, you can camp in mountain meadows. You can wade and fish in clear lakes. You can stand above roaring waterfalls plunging into deep canyons. You

ATTENTION

TRAVEL LIMITED TO
ESTABLISHED TRAIL

THE NATIONAL PARK SERVICE HAS
ESTABLISHED "BEAR MANAGEMENT AREAS"
TO REDUCE HUMAN IMPACT IN HIGH
DENSITY GRIZZLY BEAR HABITAT.

Elk and bears (insets) are among the many large
animals that live in Yellowstone National Park.

can watch bison, elk,
bears, and other wild
animals roaming free.

And at Yellowstone you
can see the world's best
display of thermal features.
Thermal means "heat." The
thermal features at

6

This colorful pool of boiling water and mud is called the Artist's Paint Pot.

Yellowstone include steaming earth, brightly colored pools of boiling water and mud, and geysers.

Geyser comes from the Icelandic word for "gusher." And that's just

7

Hot water and steam rise from the Riverside Geyser
near Firehole River in Yellowstone National Park.

what geysers do—they
gush fountains of hot
water.

The story of how
Yellowstone became a
national park is very
interesting.

8

DISCOVERY

A trapper named John Colter was the first non-Indian to visit Yellowstone. That was in 1807 or 1808.

But when later visitors— Jim Bridger, Joe Meek, Warren Angus Ferris, and Osborn Russell—talked and wrote about the wonders they had seen in Yellowstone country, no one would believe them. Bubbling pools of colored mud? Fountains that

Norris Geyser Basin

shot hot water high into the
air? Smoking earth?

People thought such things
were impossible. They
thought these visitors were
telling tall tales.

In 1835, Osborne Russell met some Shoshone living in Yellowstone. They were called sheepeaters because they hunted wild sheep for food and clothing.

In his journal, Russell wrote, "They were all neatly clothed in dressed deer and sheep skins of the best quality and seemed to be perfectly happy."

The sheepeaters were the only people who lived

Bison, or buffalo, still graze in Yellowstone.

in Yellowstone the year around. But other American Indians hunted in Yellowstone during the summer. These included Blackfeet, Crow, Flathead, and Bannock.

Ulysses S. Grant

THE WORLD'S FIRST NATIONAL PARK

Years later, when word of Yellowstone's wonders finally reached the U.S. Congress, they voted to give the area legal protection.

On March 1, 1872, President Ulysses S. Grant signed a bill that made Yellowstone the world's first national park. To be preserved were 3,384

13

Present-day Yellowstone National Park covers 3,472 square miles or 2,219,823 acres. Sights, such as the Grand Canyon of the Yellowstone River (left) and bighorn sheep (below), attract visitors.

square miles (2,165,749 acres) of some of the most beautiful country in the world.

While most of Yellowstone National Park lies in

14

Montana

Yellowstone
Park

Idaho

Wyoming

A poster of the 1890s (left) advertised the wonders of Yellowstone.

Wyoming, the western edge pushes into Idaho, and the northern border is in Montana.

Yellowstone was the start of something very good. Today, nearly 1,200 national parks exist in more than 100 countries around the world.

15

Bison (left) and moose roam the prairies and forests of Yellowstone.

In national parks there is no timber cutting, no mining, no farming, no livestock grazing, and no hunting. The parks exist to preserve nature so that people can see how the land once was, before humans changed it.

16

ANCIENT VOLCANOES

Deep in the earth, far below its hard surface crust, lies a layer of melted, or molten, rock. This liquid rock is called magma.

Sometimes, magma finds its way to the earth's surface and spews out, or erupts. When the magma flows onto the earth's surface, it is called lava. The vent, or opening in

Amphitheater Mountain rises 10,847 feet (3,306 meters) in the northeast corner of Yellowstone National Park.

the earth, from which the lava spews is called a volcano.

When lava cools on the earth's surface, it hardens into rock. Often, a cone-shaped mound of lava rock and ash forms around the vent from which it erupted. Some of these cones are as big as mountains.

Many of the landscape features in Yellowstone were formed by volcanic action.

The Sheepeater's Cliffs were named for the American Indians who once lived in Yellowstone.

In places at Yellowstone, long ago, ash from erupting volcanoes buried entire forests of trees. Over the ages, these buried trees were petrified, or turned into stone. Some of these petrified trees can still be seen at Yellowstone today.

The petrified trunk of a tree that grew in Yellowstone's ancient forest

A bison resting by one of Yellowstone's hot springs

THERMAL FEATURES

Yellowstone's volcanoes may be gone, but the thousands of hot springs and more than 200 geysers at Yellowstone show that the earth there is still very hot.

21

When water trapped underground is heated by the hot earth, it expands and turns to steam. This expansion creates pressure. The pressurized steam searches for a way out. Often, the steam bubbles up through pools of surface water. This creates a hot spring.

Bacteria and tiny plants called algae grow in many of these hot springs. It is the bacteria and algae that give Yellowstone's hot springs their

Colorful bacteria and algae growing in a hot spring (left). When a mud pot (below) is brightly colored, it is called a paint pot.

many beautiful colors—brown, yellow, orange, and green.

Sometimes, steam rises up through puddles of mud. This causes the mud to bubble and burp—*blurp! blurp!*—creating mud pots.

Midway Geyser Basin

Yellowstone has many
fumaroles. They shoot out
hot gases and steam from
holes in the earth's crust.
Fumaroles cause the
"smoking earth" that the
early visitors described and
no one would believe.

24

HOT-WATER FOUNTAINS

A geyser is like a natural hot-water fountain. When the underground energy builds to a certain point, the geyser's hot water flashes into steam. Steam and hot water blast into the air through a hole, or vent, in the earth's surface.

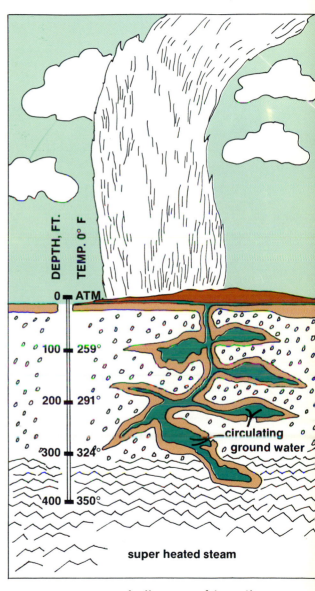

DEPTH, FT.	TEMP. 0° F
0	ATM.
100	259°
200	291°
300	324°
400	350°

circulating ground water

super heated steam

A diagram of how the Yellowstone geysers work

When a geyser runs out
of water or energy, the
eruption stops. The
heating and expansion cycle
starts all over again,
building toward another
eruption.

A geyser needs three
things: heat, water, and
a plumbing system strong
enough to stand up to the
pressures put on it during
an eruption.

The most famous
Yellowstone geyser is Old
Faithful. It "blows its

Old Faithful

top" every 40 to 100 minutes. Old Faithful erupts more regularly than any other geyser.

Each eruption of Old Faithful shoots a spout of

27

Yellowstone's thermal features are dangerous. To protect themselves from breaking through the thin crust covering the ground, visitors stay on the wooden walkways.

water from 100 to 184 feet (30 to 56 meters) into the air, and lasts about 4 minutes.

Remember that all these thermal features—geysers, hot springs, mud pots, and fumaroles—are dangerous. The ground near many of them is thin and crusty, with scalding water just below.

ICE AND WATER

Heat has played the most important role in making Yellowstone the magical place it is. But ice has been at work there too.

Much of Yellowstone's landscape was shaped by glaciers.

The Gallatin Mountains in the northwest corner of Yellowstone National Park were shaped by glaciers.

A glacier is made of
thousands of tons of ice
formed when heavy layers
of snow are pressed
together. As Yellowstone's
ancient glaciers slid slowly

In the summer, Yellowstone's valleys are full of beautiful wildflowers.

downhill and melted, they gouged out valleys and formed lakes.

There are several glacial lakes in the park. By far the biggest is Yellowstone Lake.

Yellowstone Lake has 110 miles (177 kilometers) of shoreline. It is so wide you can hardly see from one side to the other. And in places, it is as much as 390 feet (119 meters) deep.

Yellowstone Lake

The water in Yellowstone
Lake is clear and very cold.
A beautiful native trout
called the Yellowstone
cutthroat lives there.

Rivers also have helped shape the scenery at Yellowstone. A deep gorge, called the Grand Canyon of the Yellowstone,

The Yellowstone River has cut through yellow rhyolite rock to carve the Grand Canyon.

In its course, the Yellowstone River passes through the broad Hayden Valley (above) and threads its way along the narrow bottom of the Grand Canyon (opposite).

runs through the eastern part of the park. This canyon was cut by the rushing water of the Yellowstone River over thousands of years.

Yellowstone Canyon is
24 miles (38 kilometers)
long and as deep as
1,200 feet (366 meters). Of
the more than 150
permanent waterfalls in the
park, two of the best are
in Yellowstone Canyon.

Upper Yellowstone Falls
tumbles 109 feet (33
meters). Lower Yellowstone
Falls drops a dizzying
308 feet (94 meters),
foaming and roaring all the
way down.

The park's animals, such as elk (top left), moose (top right), and bison (below) are protected from hunters.

WILDLIFE

Can you imagine seeing bison (also called buffalo) walking through the place where you are having a picnic lunch? At Yellowstone National Park, it happens every day!

You also have a good chance of seeing moose and elk. Moose are the largest members of the deer family. A bull moose may weigh 900 pounds or more.

Another animal found at
Yellowstone is the pronghorn.
It likes the open country
and sagebrush.
Yellowstone Park also is

Clockwise from top left: pronghorn,
moose, grizzly bear, and black bear

Water birds such as the trumpeter swan (above) and the osprey make their home in Yellowstone.

home to both black bears and grizzly bears.

Yellowstone National Park is a great place to see water birds such as geese, gulls, and ospreys (also called fishing eagles).

41

Black bear cubs exploring their world

It is important to remember that all wild animals can be dangerous, even little cute ones. Never try to touch any wild animal. You might frighten it and cause it to injure itself—or to injure you. Respect wild animals. Always enjoy them from a

safe distance.

LAND OF GEYSERS AND GRIZZLY BEARS

While sight-seeing is great fun at Yellowstone, there are also lots of other things to do there.

You can paddle a canoe. You can take

Park visitors canoeing on the Lewis River

The Bechler River runs through the southwest corner of Yellowstone.

pictures. You can camp, picnic, hike, and ride horseback. You can even ride in a real stagecoach!

And here is the best part of all: Because Yellowstone is protected as a national park, it will

always be there, waiting
for you to visit–a magical
place of geysers and
grizzlies.

WORDS YOU SHOULD KNOW

algae (AL • jee) — tiny plants that live in water

ash (ASH) — grayish, powdery matter that comes out of a volcano

attraction (uh • TRACK • shun) — something that people come to see

canyon (KAN • yun) — a long, narrow valley that has high cliffs on each side

cycle (SY • kil) — a complete set of events that keeps repeating in the same order

eruption (ih • RUP • shun) — the sudden release of melted rock (lava), hot gases, steam, or water escaping through a crack or vent in the earth's surface.

expand (ex • PAND) — to become larger

explorer (ex • PLOR • er) — a person who travels to an unknown place to see what is there

fumarole (FOO • ma • roll) — steam and hot gases escaping from a crack or other vent in the earth's surface

geyser (GYE • zer) — a natural hot-water fountain; a geyser requires underground water, heat, and a surface vent

glacier (GLAY • sher) — a thick mass of snow and ice that moves slowly across land or down a mountain

gorge (GORJE) — a deep, rocky, narrow valley

lava (LA • va) — hot rock that comes out of a volcano

magma (MAG • ma) — melted rock deep inside the earth

osprey (AHS • pree) — a large black and white bird that feeds on fish

petrified (PET • rih • fyd) — turned into stone

preserve (prih • ZERV) — to keep safe from change or harm

pressure (PRESH • er) — a force pressing against a surface

regularly (REG • yoo • ler • lee) — not changing; at evenly spaced times

rhyolite (RY • uh • lite) — a volcanic rock

scalding (SKAWL • ding) — very hot
thermal (THER • mil) — caused by heat
vent (VENT) — an opening through which steam or lava escapes
volcano (vahl • KAY • no) — an opening in the earth's crust through which molten lava erupts

INDEX

About the Author

*David Petersen is a writer and teacher living in Colorado. He made
his first visit to Yellowstone Park when he was three years old.*